VANGUARD SERIES

EDITOR: MARTIN WINDROW

THE PANZERKAMPFWAGEN III

Text by

BRYAN PERRETT

Colour plates by

DAVID E. SMITH and MIKE CHAPPELL

OSPREY PUBLISHING LONDON

Published in 1980 by
Osprey Publishing Ltd
Member company of the George Philip Group
12–14 Long Acre, London WC2E 9LP
© Copyright 1980 Osprey Publishing Ltd

ISBN 0 85045 362 3

Filmset in Great Britain
Printed in Hong Kong

PzKpfw III Ausf. A photographed in Poland, 1939. The Ausf. A
–D were fitted with a circular hull machine gun mounting.
Note yellow turret cross; see Plate A1 and commentary.
(Bundesarchiv)

Development

On 16 March 1935 the German government formally repudiated the disarmament clauses of the Treaty of Versailles, which contained the strict proviso that Germany was prohibited from owning or obtaining tracked armoured fighting vehicles. Hitler had calculated correctly that British and French reaction to the repudiation would be limited to toothless bluster, and having thus presented the world with a *fait accompli*, set about building up his armed services by the introduction of universal conscription and the initiation of a vast arms production programme.

Although herself forbidden to manufacture tanks while the Treaty provisions applied, Germany was far from being totally lacking in tank design experience. In the years following the Great War, she had co-operated with that other contemporary international pariah, Bolshevik Russia, in establishing a secret experimental station on the Karma River, although the result of the joint research programme tended to be of

greater benefit to the Red Army; and Sweden had also provided some practical assistance.

In addition to the experimental prototypes constructed in conjunction with the Russians, two light tanks had been designed and were actually in process of manufacture under the guise of agricultural tractors when the repudiation took place. These became known as the PzKpfw I and PzKpfw II, their intended rôles being respectively training and reconnaissance. As these vehicles left the production lines they were sent immediately to the newly formed Panzer divisions as temporary expedients pending the appearance of purpose-built main battle tanks, the plan being that each battalion should consist of one Heavy Company, equipped with tanks carrying a large-calibre gun for close support, and three Medium Companies, whose tanks would carry an armour-defeating gun and two machine guns. In due course the mount of the Heavy Company would become known as the PzKpfw

3

An early Ausf. E of 3. Panzer-Regiment, 2. Panzer-Division *en route* for Greece during the 1941 Balkan campaign. Other photographs of this unit confirm the distinctive style of markings, with a small white vehicle number on the hull side well forward, tactical symbols on the turret side, and a horse-shoe displayed on the track-guard. See Plate A2 and commentary. (Bundesarchiv)

IV, and that of the Medium Companies as the PzKpfw III.

The starting point for the PzKpfw III design, as in every main battle tank design, was the gun. Senior tank officers requested a 50mm gun, a sensible provision at a time when the British were beginning to fit a 40mm 2pdr. gun into their new Cruiser tanks, and the Russians were already employing a 45mm gun in their BTs and T-26s. However, the *Heereswaffenamt*, responsible for procurement, demurred, pointing out with the backing of the Artillery Inspectorate that the infantry was already in possession of the 37mm anti-tank gun, which was in quantity production, and the obvious desirability of standardization of armour-piercing ammunition and weapons. An intelligent compromise was reached by which the tank officers accepted the 37mm, while the turret ring was to be constructed wide enough to accommodate the 50mm gun if necessary.

Having settled this question, the next step was to design the hull within the then 24-ton German bridge-loading specification. (Contemporary British designers were similarly hampered by a mandatory railway loading gauge restriction. This had the effect of limiting the width of their tanks, and thus the turret ring, and so ultimately the size of the weapon that could be mounted.) A standard layout was adopted with the engine mounted at the rear. Inside the turret the commander sat centrally beneath his cupola, with the gunner on the left of the gun breech and the loader on the right. In the forward compartment the driver was located on the left and the radio operator/hull gunner on the right, with the transmission between them. The final drive ran to the sprockets across the front of the forward compartment. This basic arrangement remained unaltered throughout the vehicle's history.

Once the prototypes had been produced and tested, Daimler-Benz were appointed to oversee development and manufacture, the essential requirements being specified as a 15-ton vehicle capable of 25mph. The true purpose of the vehicle was cloaked under the security title of Zugführerwagen or ZW ('platoon commander's vehicle');

4

but military bureaucracy being as self-perpetuating as any other kind, successive Marks carried in addition to their Ausführung letter a progressive ZW number, long after security had ceased to be an overriding consideration.

The **Ausführung A** appeared in 1936. The running gear consisted of five medium-sized roadwheels, front drive sprocket, spoked idler and two return rollers. The vehicle was powered by a 250hp 12-cylinder Maybach 108TR engine, and transmission was by means of a five-speed gearbox, which also provided one reverse gear.

The L/45 37mm main armament was mounted co-axially with twin 7.92mm machine guns behind a recessed mantlet which was vulnerable to bullet splash, while a further 7.92mm machine gun was carried in a ball mounting in the front plate of the hull. The commander's cupola was starkly simple, consisting of a slotted 'dustbin', and the turret was fitted with one-piece side hatches.

Daimler-Benz had hit their weight target by providing a maximum armour thickness of 14.5mm, but the suspension system was more suitable for commercial than military usage and the engine output was comparatively low, so that the vehicle's top speed of 20mph fell below the required specification. Ten vehicles of this type were produced.

The **Ausführung B** was broadly similar in its concept, but attempted to solve the suspension problem by employing leaf instead of coil springs, eight smaller road wheels being suspended from two horizontal spring units, while the number of return rollers was increased to three. This had the effect of raising the weight slightly to 15.9 tons, but achieved a modest increase in speed of 1.7mph.

Ausf. M, knocked out in Tunisia. The progressive up-gunning and up-armouring of the PzKpfw III are very striking if one compares this to the previous picture: note L/60 gun, spaced armour mantlet, and appliqué armour bolted across the front plate. From the Ausf. J onwards the hull machine gun mounting reverted to the round type. The turret number '6', in black trimmed with either red or yellow, probably refers to the company—this was normal practice with single-digit presentations. (RAC Tank Museum)

The chassis is of some interest in that it provided the basis for the prototype Sturmgeschütz (see Vanguard 12, *Sturmartillerie and Panzerjäger*).

Ausführung C was almost identical but provided an alternative method of leaf-spring arrangement, employing one large central unit and two smaller units fore and aft. Ausf. B and C were produced concurrently in 1937, 15 vehicles of each type being built.

Ostensibly **Ausführung D**, which appeared late in 1938, was a further variation on the eight-wheel leaf-spring suspension theme, in which the fore and aft units carried by the Ausf. C were angled slightly inwards. However, maximum armour thickness had been increased to 30mm and a more workmanlike cupola introduced, which was not only lower but which also provided latched visors for the protection of the vision

A Jock of 51st Highland Division peering through the final drive maintenance hatches of an Ausf. N knocked out on the 8th Army sector of the Tunisian front. One source has identified this as a support vehicle of the Tiger battalion, Independent Heavy Tank Bn. 501, and shows the colour as dark yellow, with the name '*Mauseauge*' in red on a strip of olive green. The same painting shows the tiger and rhomboid-S insignia of *501. Abteilung* on the front hull outside the driver's visor. The frame arrangement on the turret roof is interesting; its proportions seem unsuitable for track link stowage, and one may speculate that it was a camouflage net support.

blocks. These improvements raised the vehicle's weight to 19 tons, but the installation of a better gearbox containing an additional forward gear maintained the maximum speed obtainable on previous models. Some 29 vehicles of this type were built, and the earlier Marks were also up-armoured to the 30mm standard. Ausf. A to D all carried 120 rounds of main and 4,425 rounds of secondary armament ammunition.

1939 saw the appearance of the **Ausführung E**, which finally overcame the difficulties which had been experienced with the suspension. A robust torsion bar system was adopted, employing six small road wheels. The redesign of the running gear also incorporated a new disc idler, and the position of the three return rollers was slightly altered.

This Mark was driven by the 300hp 12-cylinder Maybach HL 120TR engine, and the manual gearbox employed on the earlier models was replaced by the Maybach Variorex pre-selector box which provided 10 forward and one reverse gears. Although the vehicle's weight was now 20 tons the more powerful engine produced a top speed of 25mph.

Changes in the turret design included the introduction of two-piece side hatches. Early examples of the production run show the retention of the twin co-axial machine guns and an internal mantlet, but as the series progressed the co-axial armament was reduced to one gun and an external mantlet was adopted. Hull escape hatches for the driver and radio operator were installed above the second and third road wheels although, again, these do not appear on the early versions. Estimates of production figures for the Ausf. E vary considerably, the most likely figure being in the region of one hundred.

The **Ausführung F** also began production in 1939, the early vehicles being almost indistinguishable from the first Ausf. Es, mounting a 37mm gun and twin machine guns behind an internal mantlet. However, on this model new ventilation ducts for the track brakes had been installed, and the covers for these were visible on the glacis plate.

By now the wisdom of the original proposal to fit a 50mm main armament had become apparent, and later vehicles in the series were fitted with the L/42 50mm gun in conjunction with a single co-axial machine gun, the mounting being protected by an external mantlet. This gun was also fitted retrospectively to the Ausf. E.

Ausführung G, which first appeared in October 1940, presented little external difference from its immediate predecessor, but possessed an improved commander's cupola. The first few vehicles mounted the 37mm main armament, but thereafter the L/42 50mm gun was fitted as standard. The Ausf. G was modified for service in North Africa by the provision of larger radiators and an additional air filter made from felt.

Experience in Poland and France had indicated that the PzKpfw III was under-armoured. A temporary method of correcting this would have been to add external plating to the vulnerable areas, but the suspension was already considered to be carrying its maximum load and a further increase in ground pressure was not thought to be desirable. It was therefore necessary to redesign the basic running gear to allow for the additional weight, and this resulted in the **Ausführung H**.

On this model the torsion bar suspension was strengthened and the track width increased from 36cm to 40cm. To compensate for this new

Gun control equipment of a PzKpfw III showing elevation and traverse handwheels, sighting telescope, and, below and left of the 'scope pad, the hand traverse selector lever. This appears to be an Ausf. N with 75mm L/24 howitzer, traversed left to 10 o'clock judging by the loader's stool and commander's foot rest at bottom right. (Imperial War Museum)

sprockets and idlers were introduced, the former having six apertures as opposed to eight circular holes, and the latter being of an eight-spoked type. Existing stocks of the old sprockets and idlers were also used in conjunction with spacer rings. The opportunity was also taken to replace the complicated Variorex pre-selector gearbox with the simpler Aphon synchromesh, which provided six forward and one reverse gears. Additional 30mm plates were fixed to the bow, driver's and stern plates, but although this increased the

Loader's view of main and co-axial armament. The muzzle-heavy 50mm L/42 gun is indicated by the counterweight ingot just discernible in the back of the spent case deflector shield, so this is presumably either an Ausf. H or early J, or an up-gunned F or G. (Imperial War Museum)

vehicle's weight to 21.6 tons the ground pressure actually showed a slight decrease, and the maximum speed remained unaltered.

The Ausf. H began entering service at the end of 1940 and was fitted with the L/42 50mm gun, for which a total of 99 rounds could be stowed, together with 3,750 rounds for the secondary armament. Like the Ausf. F and G it carried a rack of smoke bombs in a prominent box at the rear, the operation of which is described below.

The addition of *appliqué* armour could, however, only be regarded as a temporary expedient pending the production of a basic up-armoured design. This appeared in 1941 as the **Ausführung J**, which carried integral 50mm front and rear armour. An internal improvement was the provision of levers in place of the pedals which had activated the steering brakes on previous models.

Following the fall of France, Hitler, with considerable prescience, had given orders that the PzKpfw III's main armament should be the longer L/60 50mm gun. Partly because of supply

difficulties, these instructions had been ignored, so that when faced with the 76.2mm weapons of the T-34 and KV-1 in Russia the vehicle was caught badly short. Furious at this disobedience, the Führer flew into one of his rages, unfairly describing the PzKpfw III as an unsuccessful design. After the first Ausf. Js had been produced with the L/42 gun, the L/60 weapon was fitted as standard, and earlier models which were returned to Germany for refit were also up-gunned. Stowage of main armament ammunition for the L/60 gun was limited to 78 rounds.

The Ausf. J began reaching regiments at the end of 1941, by which time it was already apparent that a 50mm armour base was inadequate. In order to minimize the weight increase inevitable with the addition of further *appliqué* armour, it was decided to employ a spaced armour system, 20mm plates being mounted slightly ahead of the front plate and mantlet. This, together with the larger main armament, increased the tank's weight to 22.3 tons. In this version the vehicle was known as the **Ausführung L**.

The **Ausführung M** appeared in 1942 and closely resembled the Ausf. L. It was, however, fitted with a self-sealing exhaust system which enabled it to wade unprepared to a depth of five feet, this being located at the extreme rear of the vehicle. Two batteries of three smoke-bomb dischargers were fitted to the turret sides, arranged so as to drop a pattern ahead of the tank if fired simultaneously.

Between the end of 1941 and the spring of 1943 a total of 1,969 L/60 50mm PzKpfw IIIs were

The 'sight picture' of a PzKpfw III with 50mm gun: (1) Range plate (2) Sighting plate (3) Main armament engaging hard target at 1,000m (4) Co-axial MG engaging infantry at 400m.

built, but it had long been apparent that the design could not absorb further attempts at up-gunning and up-armouring. The rôle of the German Army's main battle tank had passed to the PzKpfw IV; and the final version of the PzKpfw III, the **Ausführung N**, was a close-support vehicle armed with the same L/24 75mm howitzer which had originally been mounted in the early models of the PzKpfw IV, and for which 64 rounds were stowed. Some 660 vehicles of this type were built, serving in the fire-support rôle with Panzer-Grenadier divisions and Tiger tank battalions.

Production of the PzKpfw III ended in August 1943, although the chassis continued to be used in the construction of assault guns. Latterly, vehicles were fitted with 5mm side skirts and the turrets were similarly girdled as a protection against hollow-charge ammunition; and a coating of *Zimmerit* anti-magnetic mine paste was applied.

Gunner's view of the turret of an L/60-armed Ausf. J; see Plate G and commentary. Note commander's voice-tube, and immediately below it a case for spare MG barrels stowed on the turret ring. Below this is the supplementary traverse handle, and beyond it, under the turret ring, a row of MG belt bags. The torsion-arm compensator can be seen between the 'scope pad and the internal gun crutch. (Martin Windrow)

Special-purpose Vehicles

An interesting variation was the **Tauchpanzer** ('diving tank'), which was designed in 1940 for the invasion of Great Britain. All openings to the exterior of the vehicle were sealed with a water-tight compound and the gap between hull and turret closed by an inflatable rubber ring. Rubber sheeting covered the commander's cupola, the mantlet and the hull machine gun, but this could be blown away from inside the vehicle by means of an electrical detonator. Air was supplied to the engine by a flexible 18-metre hose which was held on the surface by a buoy, while exhaust gases were carried upwards through two tall vertical pipes fitted with non-return valves. Maximum safe diving depth was 15 metres, and the crew's submerged endurance set at 20 minutes.

The intention was for the tanks to launch themselves from lighters and then motor ashore along the sea bed, direction being maintained by instructions passed through a radio link from the parent vessel. The design was, on the whole, successful and found a practical application at the crossing of the River Bug during Operation 'Barbarossa'. The crews were drawn from volun-

Looking forward from the loader's position in the same turret; note details of co-axial MG mounting. The forward parts of the auxiliary traverse linkage can be seen on the right, immediately inside the spare MG barrel case. Bottom right are the two housings, empty here, for the hull gunner/radio operator's receiver and transmitter. See Plate F and commentary. (Martin Windrow)

teer battalions, which were later formed into the 18th Panzer Regiment.

The Ausf. M formed the basis of a flame-throwing tank; the official designation of which was **PzKpfw III (Flam)**. The flame projector tube replaced the conventional 50mm gun in the mantlet, and was recognizable by being somewhat thicker. One hundred litres of flame liquid were stored inboard and driven through the projector tube by a two-stroke engine. By restricting bursts to two or three seconds' duration it was possible to obtain up to 80 flame-shots with a maximum range of 60 yards. The crew consisted of a commander/flame gunner, radio operator/hull gunner and driver. One hundred of these conversions were made, serving in specialist battalions 20 to 30 strong, and employed at the discretion of senior commanders.

A slightly off-beat development was the fitting of an Ausf. N onto a railway mounting to which the line of drive was passed by means of spindles. The vehicle was intended to patrol railways in Russia and keep them free from partisan interference, but the idea offered little that an armoured train did not, was extremely expensive, and did not proceed beyond the prototype phase.

The PzKpfw III was widely used for conversion to the rôle of **Panzerbefehlswagen** ('armoured command vehicle'). Versions were produced on the Ausf. D, E and H chassis, and all followed the same pattern with a fixed turret (usually bolted to the hull) mounting a dummy gun, and an unmistakable 'bedstead' loop aerial over the engine deck.

A report by the School of Tank Technology on a captured example based on an Ausf. H chassis notes that the turret roof was reinforced by an extra 15mm plate, presumably as a defence against mortar fire. The mantlet was moulded in light alloy and modelled on that of the Ausf. D.

The *Tauchpanzer*, or Diving Tank, seen here during trials for Operation 'Sea Lion'. Vehicles of this type were used successfully in the crossing of the River Bug during the initial stages of 'Barbarossa' in June 1941. (Bundesarchiv)

Radio equipment consisted of two sets mounted at the rear of the command compartment, directly above the propeller shaft and connected to the loop aerial. Two further sets were fitted to the forward hull wall, and a further two above the gearbox. Additional vision ports had been provided, and the report also noted the provision of cushioned seats and backrests of a more 'luxurious standard' than those employed in gun tanks, but the term is entirely relative.

The captured example did not contain a map table, but this would normally have been a standard fitting. Originally the Panzerbefehlswagen III was classed as a large command vehicle for use by regimental commanders and above, and there is good reason to believe that vehicles used by certain higher formation commanders contained the Enigma portable trans-coding

A *Panzerbefehlswagen* III of 15th Panzer Division, whose sign appears in red on the front trackguard. The marking of the national cross on the hull front was most unusual. (RAC Tank Museum)

device. Later in the war, as more vehicles became available, large ACVs were issued to battalion commanders.

One problem with the Panzerbefehlswagen was the easy identification provided by its distinctive loop aerial, which was replaced in 1943 by more conventional rods. Again, command vehicles were just as subject to breakdown as any other and their loss at a critical moment could have serious consequences. To provide immediate first-line replacement, regiments were from the autumn of 1942 issued with a basic PzKpfw III gun tank with addition radio facilities, this being known as the Panzerbefehlswagen III Ausf. K.

Until 1943 Panzerartillerie Forward Observation Officers performed their duties from a light half-track which, because of its vulnerability, was not entirely suitable for the task. However, in that year numbers of PzKpfw III gun tanks were specially converted for the rôle, their title being **Panzerbeobachtungswagen** ('armoured observation vehicle') **III**. In this version the main armament was stripped out and replaced by a

The flame-thrower version of the PzKpfw III closely resembled the Ausf. L and M, but was recognizable by the thicker barrel of the flame projector tube. The cylinder dimly visible at hull rear is part of the deep-wading exhaust system. (Imperial War Museum)

Forward tactical headquarters of 21st Panzer Division in the desert: left, an SdKfz 250/3 communications half-track; centre, a *Panzerbefehlswagen* III; and right, the divisional commander's Horch command car. In the original print the black/white/red command pennant is seen painted on the Horch's mudguard (right, as viewed) with the divisional sign in white left of its lower corner. Interestingly, the command tank once again has the national cross in white outline painted centrally on the hull front plate, partly obscured here by the shadow of the barrel. (Bundesarchiv)

single ball-mounted machine gun in the centre of the mantlet, a dummy gun being installed to its right. The interior contained an artillery board and duplicate radios, one netted to the main operational frequency, the other providing a rear link to the guns. The crew consisted of the FOO, his technical assistant, two radio operators and the driver, all of whom would have been artillery personnel.

Without doubt, the PzKpfw III's most notable offspring was the Sturmgeschütz or assault gun, the history, development and tactical employment of which is fully discussed in Vanguard 12, *Sturmartillerie and Panzerjäger*. Here it is only necessary to repeat that the 10,500 assault guns built destroyed more than three times their number of enemy fighting vehicles, and that the Sturmartilleristen considered themselves to be every bit as much an élite as the Panzertruppen.

In 1942 fighting within the built-up areas of Stalingrad indicated that a heavier weapon was needed than the 75mm howitzer carried by the assault gun. First choice fell on the 150mm Infantry Gun 33, which at that time was fitted to the

chassis of the PzKpfw I, PzKpfw II and 38T, some of which were grossly overloaded; moreover, the open-topped superstructures of these vehicles made them unsuitable for street-fighting.

In an attempt to overcome these difficulties, the chassis of the PzKpfw III was used as the basis for an experimental vehicle known as the **Sturm-Infanteriegeschütz 33**. Layout followed that of the assault gun, the weapon being mounted in a fixed enclosed superstructure with 80mm frontal armour. The vehicle weighed 22 tons, was manned by a crew of five, and had a maximum speed of 12mph; 30 rounds of main armament ammunition were carried. In the event the design was overtaken by the heavy assault gun Brummbär, which was based on the PzKpfw IV chassis. Production of the Sturm-Infanteriegeschütz 33 terminated in November 1942, by which time only 24 vehicles had been produced. They are reported as having equipped the 9th Company of Panzer Regiment 201 during the summer of 1943.

Other PzKpfw III variants included a very simple recovery vehicle, the **Bergepanzerwagen III**, which consisted of a turretless hull fitted with towing attachments; and a supply carrier, the **Schlepper III**, which carried a large wooden box superstructure in place of the turret. Turretless versions also carried ammunition in the forward zone, and the heavy equipment required by the Panzer divisions' assault engineer units. Experiments were carried out with a prototype mine-clearing vehicle, which achieved extra ground clearance by means of extension arms, but very few details are available.

By September 1941 PzKpfw III and PzKpfw IV were performing a similar battlefield rôle, and as the two designs had much in common it was felt that numerous benefits, including standardization of parts, would accrue if they were to be merged. The composite vehicle was given the title of **PzKpfw III/IV**, and several prototypes were constructed in which the parentage of the hull and turret was clearly identifiable, although the suspension now carried six large interleaved wheels. The design was ingenious but became a casualty in the accelerating gun/armour race, and was finally abandoned in 1944.

PzKpfw III Described

Armour
In April 1943 Messrs William Beardmore & Co. Ltd. of Glasgow analysed several samples of the armour plate used to construct the PzKpfw III, the consultants drawing the following conclusions:

'All the material has been made in the electric furnace and the compositions vary considerably, possibly because of different sources of supply. In every case the Carbon content is higher than is used here, whilst the combination of high Silicon and high Chromium is rather an unusual feature. The physical properties approximate to our own bullet-proof material but as a whole it does not

The German Army relied on verbal orders to a greater extent than other armies, thus accelerating the command process considerably. Here two *Panzerbefehlswagen* III have met for an orders group in Russia; while senior officers confer with maps, lesser mortals such as drivers remove themselves to a respectful distance. (Bundesarchiv)

show any improvement over this. With regard to the welding which is present at various points, this is extremely poor in all cases.'

These comments were amplified by the Ministry of Supply following detailed examination of the hull and turret of a captured Ausf. J:

'The problem of making a battle-worthy structure in this comparatively high carbon armour, using hard-surfacing and austenitic electrodes and at the same time giving assistance to the welds by means of rabbeted plate edges, *was not overcome*. The extent of cracking suggests that pre-heating was not adopted. Judged by any standards, the behaviour of the welding is unsatisfactory.'

Automotive
The Maybach engine had been designed to operate in temperate climates, in which it performed satisfactorily. However, in tropical or dusty conditions it was subject to breakdown and overheating, and a British intelligence summary dated 18 February 1942, prepared after examination of abandoned vehicles, commented on the number of failures due to engine and bogie problems.

'The engine trouble was due chiefly to sand

The armoured artillery observation vehicle, *Panzerbeobachtungswagen* III, was easily recognizable by its off-centre dummy gun; effective armament was limited to a single ball-mounted machine gun in the centre of the mantlet. (Imperial War Museum)

blocking oil supply pipes damaging crankshafts and pistons, and sand in the distributor, dynamo and starter. The air filter is entirely inadequate. Bogie trouble was due to the disintegration of tyres due to high speed or heat.'

The user handbook recommended a maximum engine speed of 2,600rpm for normal usage, but in hot climates, which included southern Russia as well as North Africa, it was suggested that employment of a lower gear than was necessary would produce cooler running. Use of the engine as a brake was permissible at 2,200–2,400rpm, but was to be avoided in the 2,600–3,300rpm band. Overheated engines tended to 'diesel' after being switched off, a fault which could be corrected by switching on again and either opening the throttle or idling until the temperature dropped. The principal components in the cooling system were two radiators with a total effective are of $5\frac{1}{2}$ square feet, through which air was dragged by two fans.

The Variorex pre-selector gearbox was considered to be effective up to seventh gear, after which the tractive effort fell away sharply. The eighth gear was suitable for level road-running, but the ninth and tenth gears were regarded as overdrives and seldom used. The Aphon synchromesh gearbox drew favourable comment, although once again the tractive effort in top (i.e. sixth) gear was low, and this was largely reserved for road use. For both systems it was recommended that 'when changing to a lower gear on turnings, hills or bad roads, *two* gears lower than the one already engaged should be selected.'

The final drive and steering brake assembly was extremely complicated. An excessive number of ball races were incorporated and, as already mentioned, considerable care was taken to provide an air cooling system for the track brake drums. Even so, there was no automatic equalization of the torque on the two output shafts, and the mechanism did not provide positive steering when both steering brakes were released.

The torsion bar suspension was adequate, although in sandy areas grit tended to penetrate the shock absorbers, shortening their life. Track tension was achieved by means of a bell crank. On the Eastern Front track extensions known as *Ostketten* were fitted to increase traction during the winter months, usually to one track only— a most dangerous practice in any sort of hilly country.

An electric self-starter was provided, but this was for use in emergency only, and never with a cold engine. The normal method of starting was by means of an inertia system, the starting handle entering the engine compartment through the tail plate. The handle was swung by two men until the flywheel had reached 60rpm, when the power was tripped to turn the main engine. The inertia starter was geared, but its operation in the depths of the Russian winter, with sump oil chilled to the consistency of treacle, required a great deal of initial effort, although the driver could eliminate the additional drag of the gearbox oil by depressing his clutch. Cold starting was assisted by a starter carburettor which was not to be used in conjunction with the accelerator. Minimum unassisted working temperature for the engine was 50 degrees Centigrade at 2,000rpm with an oil pressure of not less than 60lb per square inch.

Gunnery and Optical

Elevation of the main and co-axial armament was by means of a handwheel operated with the gunner's left hand. Immediately to the right of this was the traversing handwheel, which included a release latch and which was sometimes linked under the gun to a hand crank which could be turned by the loader. The traverse mechanism incorporated two gears, one requiring 88 turns of the handwheel to achieve a complete revolution of the turret, and the other, used for fine laying, 132 turns. The main armament was fired electrically and its recoil was controlled by a hydro-pneumatic buffer system containing a filling liquid which was simply known as Braun.

The 50mm guns carried by the PzKpfw III were muzzle heavy in their mounting. In the case of the L/42 model, this was easily corrected by the addition of a lead weight to the rear of the spent case deflector shield. However, the imbalance became even more pronounced when the longer L/60 model was fitted, and to compensate for this a small compression spring in a cylinder was mounted on the forward offside corner of the turret ring and attached to the gun. This arrangement was found on the Ausf. J, but on later Marks a torsion bar was bolted across the turret roof and connected to the upper part of the gun mounting. On later Marks, too, the recoil shield arms were $4\frac{1}{2}$in. longer, providing additional compensation but reducing clearance to the turret ring to $17\frac{1}{2}$in.

The *Bergepanzerwagen* III was a simple turretless towing vehicle; foul-weather protection was provided by a collapsible canvas hood, propped open in this Russian winter scene. (Bundesarchiv)

The sighting telescope was more complicated than its British counterpart, which employed a simple graticule pattern, and contained two movable plates. The first or range plate rotated about its own axis, the main armament and machine gun scales being marked on opposing quadrants; the 50mm scale was marked from 0 to 2,000 metres, and the machine gun scale from 0 to 800 metres. The second or sighting plate moved in a vertical plane and contained the

sighting and aim-off markings. The two plates moved simultaneously, the sighting plate rising or falling as the range plate turned. To engage at a selected range, the range wheel was turned until the required marking was opposite the pointer at the top of the sight, and the sighting mark laid onto the target by the traverse and elevation controls.

Ammunition stowage in vehicles fitted with the L/42 50mm gun was as follows:

Under the gunner's seat: 5 rounds
In locker situated at right/rear of fighting compartment: 22 rounds
In locker immediately above: 12 rounds
In locker situated at left/rear of fighting compartment: 36 rounds
In locker immediately above: 24 rounds
Total: 99 rounds.

With the exception of the rounds under the gunner's seat, all ammunition was stowed vertically, the case fitting into a recess in the locker floor while the nose was held in place by a spring clip. The arrangement was neat, but made withdrawal of certain rounds difficult. The right lower locker and two left/rear lockers were closed by sliding doors, which tended to jam with sand particles; the right upper locker was fitted with a hinged door. On L/60 50mm vehicles a horizontal stowage pattern was adopted for ready-use rounds.

Whatever system was employed, the loader laboured under something of a disadvantage in that the turret floor was fixed and he was forced to 'walk after' the gun breech whenever the turret was traversed. The commander and gunner were more fortunate in that their seats were attached to the turret itself.

Machine gun ammunition was distributed along the walls of the fighting and hull gunner's compartments in bags, each bag containing a 150-round belt. The bag system was less efficient than the British metal box 'liner', and required one hand to assist passage of the belt into the gun. In consequence, while the hull gunner could traverse by using the pistol grip of his weapon, elevation and depression were extremely difficult. The problem was resolved by the novel method of the hull gunner inserting his head into a moulded rubber cap which was linked to the butt of the machine gun by a bar; he could then lower his head to obtain elevation, and raise it for depression.

Some mention has already been made of the smoke-bomb rack, which was prominent on the rear of Ausf. F, G and H. On later models, pending the introduction of turret dischargers, this device was concealed beneath the engine air-outlet cowling. The rack carried five bombs, held in position by spring-loaded catches. The vehicle commander released the bombs singly by a wire control which operated a ratchet wheel coupled to a camshaft. Each pull of the wire rotated the camshaft one-fifth of a turn, releasing a bomb, the pin of which was drawn by a fixed chain, and the ratchet was returned by a second spring. Thus, five pulls on the control wire would release

all the bombs in succession, enabling the tank to reverse out of sight into its own smoke screen.

The design of the commander's cupola incorporated armoured shutters which could be latched in the open, intermediate or closed positions to protect the safety-glass vision blocks. Some commanders had a clock code painted round the inside of their cupolas to remind them of the turret's position in relation to the hull, a thing sometimes forgotten in the heat of action.

In normal circumstances the driver employed a direct-vision safety-glass block. In action this could be covered by a latched slab, its place being taken by a pair of periscopic binoculars, the two ports for which were visible directly above the visor. The German safety-glass of the period had a slightly greenish tinge.

An unusual picture of the PzKpfw III/IV, of which very few were constructed. Different types of wheel have been employed for the inner and outer halves of the interleaved suspension, and one of the latter appears to have been damaged. The tank is being used here as a 'dozer. (Imperial War Museum)

Organization and Tactics

The principal component of the Panzer division was, of course, its tank element. The establishment envisaged for the original Panzer divisions contained two two-battalion regiments, each battalion consisting of four 32-tank companies. Together with armoured command vehicles, this gave the Panzer division a total tank strength of 561—a dream which never approached realization.

Despite the re-armament programme, German tank production in the immediate pre-war years was sluggish and in September 1939 the majority of battalions possessed only five PzKpfw IIIs, sufficient to equip one platoon, a total of 20 per division. The balance of the divisional tank strength consisted of 24 PzKpfw IVs and light PzKpfw Is and IIs, supplemented in some cases by the recently acquired Czech 35Ts and 38Ts. Even so, the average number of tanks in the division was 320, so that battalions were forced to leave their fourth companies, i.e. 25 per cent of their paper strength, behind in their depots.

By May 1940 the situation had improved sufficiently for each of the divisions of Guderian's XIXth Panzer Corps to be equipped with 90 PzKpfw IIIs and 36 PzKpfw IVs, the divisional strength being fleshed out with PzKpfw Is and IIs. Other divisions had an establishment of 50 PzKpfw IIIs and 24 PzKpfw IVs, plus the lighter German models. Those divisions (6th, 7th and 8th) whose primary armament consisted of 37mm-armed Czech vehicles do not seem to have received an official allocation of PzKpfw IIIs, but Rommel's 7th Panzer Division certainly acquired several, since he records the loss of six during the fighting at Arras on 21 May. Overall divisional strengths varied between 218 and 276 tanks, about half the theoretical establishment.

Following the startling success achieved in France, Hitler decided to double the number of Panzer divisions. This was achieved by halving the tank element, which was reduced to a single regiment of two battalions, although six regiments had a three-battalion establishment. By now the PzKpfw I and the 35T were considered obsolete, but the PzKpfw II was still employed

The Panzer III fared very badly in its first encounters with the British Matilda. Prodigious efforts to increase their protection with bogies and track links did not save this crew, apparently. (Imperial War Museum)

for reconnaissance and there were sufficient PzKpfw IIIs to equip two 22-tank companies in each battalion. At the time of the invasion of Russia divisional strength varied between 150 and 200 tanks.

1942 saw a further rise in the number of Panzer divisions in spite of the losses of the previous year and the slow growth in tank production. On the Eastern Front the northern and central sectors remained relatively quiescent, and regiments possessed equipment for a single battalion only. On the active southern sector the number of tank battalions was increased to three, but in practical terms this meant a mere 170 tanks.

At this stage it was decided to increase the number of battalion companies to four, the old pre-war figure, but in the majority of cases the equipment was simply not available to implement the directive. Indeed, following the Stalingrad campaign and the withdrawal from the Caucasus, the average Panzer division possessed about 27 tanks.

During 1943 the PzKpfw III declined rapidly in importance as a battle tank, its place being taken by the improved PzKpfw IV and the PzKpfw V Panther, although the close-support Ausf. N continued to support Panzer-Grenadier operations.

The Panzer division was designed purely for offensive operations with its armoured regiment acting as its spearhead. A comparatively narrow sector of front, varying in width between 3,000 and 5,000 yards, was selected for its attack, the tanks' firepower being concentrated in a *keil* or wedge, each wave of which was allotted the destruction of some aspect of the defence. The sheer weight of the attack would generally take the tanks through the defended zone and they would then accelerate towards their strategic objective, covering up to 60 miles a day.

In their wake would come the motorized rifle regiments, later called Panzer-Grenadiers, who would mop up any by-passed centres of resistance and hold selected areas of captured ground; the anti-tank units, which would form Pakfronts against counter-attacks; the mechanized artillery batteries, ready to support the tanks with fire against specific strong points which were delaying their advance; the divisional service units, with their maintenance, supply and replenishment facilities; while within easy reach of their ground controller the *Stukageschwader* circled, ready to pounce down on pinpoint targets in their rôle as flying artillery.

Concentration and continual movement were the twin pillars of Panzer division tactics. Concentration, because the intention was to have more barrels in the gun line at the point of contact than the enemy; and continual movement, because once a breakthrough had been achieved the enemy commander would be unable to react quickly with effective counter-measures against a mobile force whose location remained uncertain.

If a heavily defended zone was reached it was by-passed, encircled and left for the follow-up troops, i.e. the infantry divisions, while the advance continued. In the event of an armoured counter-attack the Panzers would fight together, and if the engagement began to go against them would adopt defensive/offensive tactics, retiring behind their own anti-tank gun screen, returning to the attack once the enemy armour had blunted its potential against this. Should it be necessary to carry out a tactical withdrawal this was undertaken by alternate bounds, the tanks working in conjunction with their anti-tank gunners.

It was, of course, the universal provision of radios which permitted this degree of flexibility, but the German Army also set much store on the personal initiative of the commanders on the spot. Command was exercised from among the division's leading elements, and more reliance was placed upon spoken as opposed to written orders than in other armies. In addition, German commanders were adept in the rapid formation of *ad hoc* battlegroups for special operations, using any troops which happened to be immediately available.

PzKpfw III in Action

Poland
For the Polish campaign, which began on 1 September 1939, only 98 PzKpfw IIIs Ausf. A–E were available, the main burden of the fighting falling on the 1,445 PzKpfw Is and 1,223 PzKpfw IIs, supported by 211 PzKpfw IVs.

The German strategy for the campaign involved a twin double encirclement of the Polish armies defending the western frontier of their country, the first pincers being designed to close around the forward armies in their defences while the second penetrated deep into the hinterland to isolate the reserve armies which were forming. In this design the planners were materially assisted by geography, East Prussia already lying along the Poles' northern flank while the German occupation of Czechoslovakia had given them a similar advantage in the south.

Against the seven Panzer and four light armoured divisions available to the Wehrmacht, the Polish Army could oppose only 190 tanks, the majority based on the Vickers 6-ton design, and 470 more or less useless machine gun-armed tankettes; most of these vehicles were distributed among the infantry and cavalry divisions, where they could play only a subordinate rôle. In such circumstances defeat was inevitable, but what unhinged the Polish command system with such rapidity was the deep penetration rôle of the German armour, which in all fairness could not have been predicted.

Once through the defended zone the Panzer divisions, aided by heavy tactical air support, inflicted casualties and caused grave confusion, completing their encirclements entirely according to plan. By the time Russia intervened the

A posed photograph of British infantry inspecting a broken-down PzKpfw III in the desert. To the right of the single turret number, the palm tree insignia of the *DAK* can just be made out, above a cluster of water canteens. This obviously experienced crew had acquired all kinds of useful impedimenta; but far more serviceable for water stowage would have been British-style *chagals*, the canvas bags which kept water cool by evaporation. (Imperial War Museum)

Polish Army had ceased to exist as an organized entity.

It was not, however, quite the free ride the world thought it to be at the time. This was the first occasion on which the Panzer divisions were committed *en masse*, and there were unforeseen difficulties, both tactical and logistic, which were encountered for the first time. For example, Guderian, whose XIXth Panzer Corps had motored across the Polish Corridor into East Prussia and then swung south into the enemy's heartland, had to apply considerable 'stick' to sub-units which became shy at the thought of a continuous drive so deep into hostile territory. On 9 September 4th Panzer Division learned the sharp lesson that tanks have only a limited rôle to play in street-fighting, being ejected from Warsaw with the loss of 60 of its Panzers. Throughout, dug-in anti-tank guns caused fearful havoc among the ranks of the thinly-armoured PzKpfw

Is, and perhaps the most significant pointer to emerge from the campaign was that no assault on the West could be contemplated before the numbers of PzKpfw IIIs had risen appreciably. Luckily for Germany, the British and French left her unmolested to complete her preparations.

France and the Low Countries

On 10 May 1940 German tank strength consisted of 523 PzKpfw Is, 955 PzKpfw IIs, 349 PzKpfw IIIs, 278 PzKpfw IVs, 106 35Ts and 288 38Ts, a total of 2,499 tanks. In addition, 96 PzKpfw Is had been converted as command vehicles for

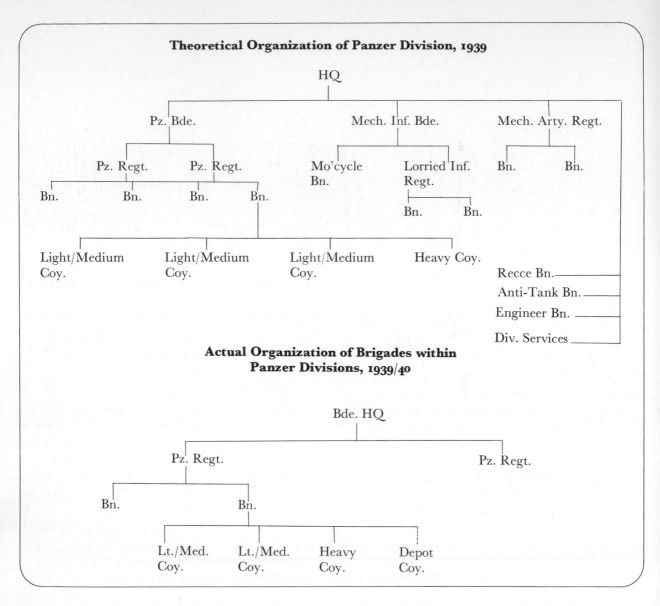

Theoretical Organization of Panzer Division, 1939

HQ
- Pz. Bde.
  - Pz. Regt.
    - Bn.
    - Bn.
  - Pz. Regt.
    - Bn.
    - Bn.
  - Light/Medium Coy.
  - Light/Medium Coy.
  - Light/Medium Coy.
  - Heavy Coy.
- Mech. Inf. Bde.
  - Mo'cycle Bn.
  - Lorried Inf. Regt.
    - Bn.
    - Bn.
- Mech. Arty. Regt.
  - Bn.
  - Bn.
- Recce Bn.
- Anti-Tank Bn.
- Engineer Bn.
- Div. Services

Actual Organization of Brigades within Panzer Divisions, 1939/40

Bde. HQ
- Pz. Regt.
  - Bn.
  - Bn.
    - Lt./Med. Coy.
    - Lt./Med. Coy.
    - Heavy Coy.
    - Depot Coy.
- Pz. Regt.

lower formations, while 39 Panzerbefehlswagen IIIs had been provided for senior commanders, a clear indication that the Army as a whole was going to be led from the front.

Opposing them were 3,285 first-line French tanks of various designs, manned by an army which contemporary world opinion considered to be the true experts in armoured warfare. However, over one-third of these vehicles were distributed along the front in direct support of infantry and horsed cavalry divisions, rather like beads on a string, and could be excluded from any plan involving concerted reaction *en masse*. The French did in fact possess a number of armoured formations, of which the most experienced were the three *Divisions Légères Méchaniques* (DLM) composed of mechanized cavalry regiments, and the lessons of the Polish campaign had led to the hasty formation of four armoured divisions known as *Divisions Cuirassées* (DCR), which had barely settled down as integrated formations. The functions of the DLMs and DCRs each covered certain aspects of the Panzer divisions' potential, the former performing the traditional cavalry rôle of reconnaissance and advanced screen, while the latter's primary task was breaching the enemy's defensive crust; but neither had been designed, nor were mentally prepared for continuous fast-moving operations in the German manner. Their principal armament consisted respectively of the Somua medium tank with its 47mm gun, 56mm armour and top speed of 25mph, and the Char B heavy tank with a 37mm gun in the turret, a 75mm in the hull, 60mm armour and a speed of 17.5mph, both backed by Hotchkiss H35 light tanks, which were armed with a 37mm gun and carried 34mm armour.

At the time, the only armoured formation serving with the British Expeditionary Force was 1st Army Tank Brigade, equipped with 74 Mark I and II Matilda Infantry tanks, protected by 60mm and 78mm armour, the latter being armed with a 2pdr. gun which was marginally superior to the German 37mm. The remainder of the British armour consisted of the thin-skinned light tanks of the infantry's divisional cavalry regiments.

Thus, save in the area of light tanks, the Germans were out-numbered, out-gunned and under-armoured, and it was clear from the outset that in the inevitable tank-versus-tank fighting the burden would fall heavily on the 37mm-armed vehicles, and specifically on the PzKpfw IIIs, which carried slightly heavier armour than the Czech tanks.

On the other hand the apparent technical superiority of the French tanks was more than off-set by the adoption of a one-man turret system. This meant that the vehicle commander was something of a one-man band, directing his driver, selecting ground on which to fight, loading, laying and firing the main armament and, if an officer, trying to control the other vehicles under his command as well. Few men can cope success-

A rare photograph taken during the height of the Sidi Rezegh fighting; in the foreground is a PzKpfw III completely wrecked by a direct hit from—probably—a 25pdr. shell, which has blown off three road wheels and two return rollers, stripped the drive sprocket, torn out a torsion arm, and blown the track clear of the vehicle. In the background is a knocked-out British 2pdr. portee (see Vanguard 10, *Allied Tank Destroyers*). (Col. P. W. H. Whiteley, OBE, TD)

fully with such uncompromising and simultaneous pressures, which presented a marked contrast to the smoothly efficient drill being executed in the turrets of the PzKpfw IIIs, and in consequence the standard of French tactical performance was well below that of the German.

The course of the 1940 campaign in France is too well known to require repetition here in detail. Briefly, the Allies expected the German Army to repeat the Schlieffen Plan, which had almost succeeded in 1914, and anticipated a 'right hook' through the Low Countries to unhinge their left, the last phase of the plan seeing them swept back against the Maginot Line in a gigantic encirclement. Such a scheme had been in the collective mind of OKW, but was replaced by a more imaginative concept based on the first of Ludendorff's 1918 *Kaiserschlacht* offensives, aimed at Amiens and the Somme estuary, the possession of which would have the effect of completely isolating the Allied armies in the north from those in the south. The thrust would be directed through the Ardennes, which were not covered by the Maginot defences since the French believed, wrongly, that the thickly wooded hills were tank-proof. The plan was conceived by von Manstein, considered to be the Army's best operational brain,

Organization of Light/Medium Panzer Company, 1940/41*

Coy. HQ
(2 × PzKpfw III)

1st Platoon   2nd Platoon   3rd Platoon   4th Platoon

(Up to 6 × PzKpfw I or II)   (Up to 6 × PzKpfw I or II,   (3 × PzKpfw III)   (3 × PzKpfw III)
or 3 × PzKpfw III)

*In practice organization varied widely, depending upon available equipment.

and given the name *Sichelschnitt* (Sickle Cut). In the meantime, it would do no harm to permit the Allies to believe that the old Schlieffen strategy was to be implemented, since it would draw away their reserves from the break-in sector and actually increase the number of troops caught in the trap, and for that reason an invasion of Holland and Belgium became a necessity.

When the offensive opened on 10 May the Allies reacted exactly as OKW had hoped, 1st and 7th French Armies and the BEF racing north to assist the hard-pressed Dutch and Belgians. Three days later the 3rd DLM, possibly the most effective of the French armoured formations, was acting as an advance screen while 1st Army moved into pre-determined defensive positions, and fought a hard encounter battle with 4th Panzer Division in the Gembloux Gap.

The Germans were aided by their dive-bombers, which further distracted the already harrassed French vehicle commanders, and were able to concentrate their tanks against the more dispersed enemy sub-units; but nevertheless their attack was held. The battle raged throughout the day, each side losing about 100 tanks, but many of the German vehicles were recovered when the French withdrew during the evening. (The possession of, or freedom to manoeuvre on a battlefield littered with abandoned tanks at the end of the day was to be a factor of great importance throughout the war—a factor initially appreciated by the Germans more readily than the Allies.)

Ironically, both sides achieved their objects.

3rd DLM ensured that 1st Army settled into its positions unmolested, and the weight of 4th Panzer Division's attack had convinced the French High Command that the major German thrust was, after all, being directed through the Low Countries.

The potentially powerful 1st and 2nd DCRs had been ordered to move north to Charleroi to counter this when Panzergruppe von Kleist, organized in two corps with a total of five Panzer divisions, burst out of the Ardennes, and the real German intentions became apparent. The two French formations were immediately ordered south to deal with the threat.

There is an ancient military maxim that the only product of order followed by counter-order is disorder, and never was the truth of this more cruelly demonstrated than on this occasion. The major French counter-attack force achieved the almost impossible feat of travelling in several directions simultaneously, its fighting elements in some instances separated from their vital supply echelons by the width of a river. Long before they could come to grips with von Kleist, they were bundled aside by Hoth's XVth Panzer Corps (5th and 7th Panzer Divisions) in a series of running fights which did nothing to slow the speed of the German advance. The formidable Char Bs found themselves committed to action almost by accident, in small groups which were desperately short of fuel and without any coherent operational control. At first their appearance was unnerving, for their guns could knock out every tank in the German armoury while their stout frontal armour withstood the return 37mm fire with ease. However, after the initial shock had been overcome, German tactical expertise ensured that superior firepower, both ground and aerial, was mustered against each of the French vehicles, while tank gunners began to pick their shots with care; a shattered track would deprive a Char B of lateral as well as forward movement, so inhibiting the use of its 75mm hull-mounted gun, while a flank shot through the prominent radiator louvres would destroy the vehicle. In addition, numbers of Char Bs, their fuel tanks dry, were abandoned and set on fire by their crews to prevent capture. By the end of this sequence of encounters 1st and 2nd DCRs had ceased to count.

German armoured columns were now cutting a 30-mile swathe across France. On 15 May the 3rd DCR attempted to counter-attack the flank of this corridor south of Sedan, but was hindered by ambivalent orders, stalled, and was finally destroyed in detail. The following day the 4th DCR, commanded by Charles de Gaulle, attacked farther west at Montcornet, and although it was successfully contained by 10th Panzer Division, it none the less made sufficient impression to raise serious doubts in the minds of OKH and OKW.

The fact was that the Germans had not escaped these encounters uninjured; furthermore the continuous running was beginning to take its toll in the form of breakdowns, and the number of PzKpfw IIIs, upon which the Army relied for its cutting edge, was dwindling. Again, to many senior officers it seemed as though the Panzer divisions were driving straight into a trap which would clang shut as the bulk of the French armour closed in across their rear. This view overestimated not only the capability of the French armoured force, still playing a subordinate supportive rôle many miles behind the real battlefront, but also the capacity of the enemy High Command for rapid response. However, these views could not be ignored and the doubts they raised led to heated exchanges between thrusting commanders like Guderian and his more conservative superiors. After serious consideration the advance was allowed to continue, and on 19 May Amiens was captured and the Allied armies were cut in two.

Two days later it seemed to worried officers at OKW that the anticipated thunder-bolt had fallen. Near Arras the British 1st Army Tank Brigade launched a counter-attack which sliced 7th Panzer Division in half and put the SS Division *'Totenkopf'* to flight. By evening the situation had been restored with the assistance of the Luftwaffe, but Rommel's immediate report maintained that he had been attacked by 'hundreds' of tanks, a wild exaggeration which led to the halting of the Panzer drive against the Channel Ports and even the despatch of several formations back along their own tracks to deal with the crisis.

By the time it was resumed, the Allies had recovered their balance sufficiently to organize the Dunkirk evacuation, throughout which the German armour was mistakenly held back while the Luftwaffe, at Göring's jealous request, attempted and failed to deliver the *coup de grâce*.

After a short period of rest and reorganization the Wehrmacht turned its attention to those Allied forces which had formed a new front south of the original Panzer corridor. Such French armoured formations as still existed were in no condition to resist for long, and although the British 1st Armoured Division had landed at Cherbourg it had been scrambled together so hastily that guns, sights, ammunition and radios were all in short supply; it was, as its commander put it, a travesty of an armoured division, whose true potential was reflected by the plywood superstructure of its 'armoured' command vehicle.

The French relied on defence in depth with numerous carefully sited artillery killing grounds. These took their toll until the guns were silenced by the Luftwaffe, and then the Panzer divisions streamed south through the gaps in the broken front with nothing to stop them. The 1st Armoured Division fought a number of delaying actions but was outflanked and forced to withdraw to Cherbourg, whence it was evacuated. On 22 June France concluded an armistice with Germany.

The campaign had been won by brilliant teamwork between the Luftwaffe and the spearheads of the Panzer divisions, aided by French demoralization and obsolete tactical doctrines. At a cost of only 156,000 German casualties, of whom 60,000 were killed, Holland, Belgium and France had been conquered and the British Army forced to leave the mainland of Europe, abandoning its heavy equipment. Allied casualties totalled 2,300,000, and the huge French armoured force was all but eliminated.

But for the Panzer divisions which had done most of the fighting, the victory had not been cheap—in fact it had cost them almost half their tanks, mainly of the lighter type, from various causes. Another point which was obscured in the general euphoria was that the divisional workship facilities had been under increasing strain towards the end, a problem that was deceptively eased by back-loading the worst breakdowns and battle casualties to Germany; in a larger context, this absence of heavy repair facilities would have most serious consequences.

For the designers of the PzKpfw III the campaign in the West represented their greatest triumph, and entirely vindicated the German concept of a main battle tank. True, the Char Bs and the Somuas had provided some anxious moments (the British Matildas had barely been encountered in the tank-versus-tank context), and for this reason the vehicle was up-gunned with a 50mm main armament, as we have already seen.

North Africa

That the German Army was present at all in this improbable theatre was due to the shattering defeat inflicted on the Italians by Wavell's 'Thirty Thousand' during late 1940 and early 1941. Sent by Hitler to bolster his shaky ally with strictly limited resources and an equally limited brief, Generalleutnant Erwin Rommel, former commander of 7th Panzer Division, discovered a weakness in the British dispositions at Mersa Brega and, contrary to his orders, attacked on 31 March 1941. The attack broke through the flimsy defensive screen and the ruthless exploitation that followed compelled the evacuation not only of the Benghazi bulge but of the whole of Cyrenaica, with the exception of the port of Tobruk. By 13 April the Axis forces were on the Egyptian frontier and had taken the strategically important Halfaya Pass.

On 19 April an attempt was made to penetrate the Tobruk perimeter. The Australian infantry let the leading PzKpfw IIIs pass over them and then engaged the follow-up troops, who were compelled to go to ground. The German tanks were then subjected to fire from the hull-down Cruisers of 'B' and 'C' Squadrons 1st Royal Tank Regt. and the Matildas of 'D' Squadron,

1. PzKpfw III Ausf.A, 2.Panzer-Division, Poland, 1939
2. PzKpfw III Ausf.E, 2.Panzer-Division, Balkans, 1941
3. PzKpfw III Ausf.J, 14.Panzer-Division, Russia, 1941

A

1. PzKpfw III Ausf.G, DAK, Libya, 1941
2. PzKpfw III Ausf.J, ex-21.Panzer-Division, North Africa, 1942
3. PzKpfw III Ausf.N, 15.Panzer-Division, Tunisia, 1942-43

B

DAVID E SMITH

1. PzKpfw III Ausf.H, 10.Panzer-Division, Russia, 1941-42

2. PzKpfw III Ausf.J, 24.Panzer-Division, Russia, 1942

C

1. PzKpfw III Ausf.M, thought to be of 3.SS-Panzer-Division 'Totenkopf', Kursk, 1943

2. PzKpfw III Ausf.J, 1.SS-Panzer-Division 'Leibstandarte Adolf Hitler', Russia, 1943

D

DAVID E SMITH

1

1. PzKpfw III Ausf.M, command tank, unidentified artillery unit, Russia, 1943-44

2. PzKpfw III Ausf.L, 3.SS-Panzer-Division 'Totenkopf', Kursk, July 1943

2

DAVID E SMITH

E

(Top) Driving compartment interior, PzKpfw III Ausf.J — see key on p.25
(Bottom) Radio operator/hull gunner's position, PzKpfw III Ausf.J

F

MIKE CHAPPELL

(Top) Commander's position, PzKpfw III Ausf.J — see key on p.25
(Bottom) Turret interior, PzKpfw III Ausf.J

1. Private, Army Panzertruppen, 1939-40
2. Panzer crewman, Russia, summer 1941
3. Panzer crewman, Deutsches Afrika Korps, 1942
4. Panzer crewman, 3.SS-Panzer-Division
   'Totenkopf', 1942-43

MIKE CHAPPELL

Key, Plate F (top): PzKpfw III Ausf. J driving compartment interior:

1 Hull left-side vision block device—note greenish tinge to visor glasses
2 Electrically driven gyroscope direction indicator
3 Spare microphone stowage
4 Driver's vision block device with armoured binocular swung over it, hinging at right-hand edge (*Fahrersehklappe 50, Fahreroptik KFF 2*).
5 Tensioning lever and tensioning spring
6 Instrument panel. Large dial at left is rev. indicator; two small dials top centre are speedometer and oil pressure; water temperature below speedometer; fuses at bottom right.
7 Gear lever
8 Starter carburettor control
9 Seat cushion
10 Steering levers
11 Final drive housing
12 Spares stowage for *KFF 2* vision device
13 Gas mask stowage
14 MG belt bag stowage

Plate F (bottom): Radio operator/hull gunner's compartment:

15 Ball-mounted hull MG, with head-pad elevation mechanism
16 MG belt bag stowage
17 Hull right-side vision block device
18 MG belt bags in place
19 Seat back—flat box of MG tools usually stowed on rear face
20 Transmitter, covered here by swung-up folding table
21 MG monocular sight
22 Receiver

Key, Plate G (top): PzKpfw III Ausf. J commander's position:

1 Cupola; vision blocks have sliding steel covers operated by bars on quadrants.
2 Pistol port handles
3 Counterweight ingot in rear of L/42 gun shellcase deflector shield
4 Gas mask stowage
5 Commander's seat on turret ring cradle; water-bottle stowage behind.
6 Spare vision block stowage
7 Seat back support on turret rear wall; stowage for flare pistol, headset, etc., behind.

Plate G (bottom): Turret interior, looking forward and left:

8 Internal gun crutch
9 Extractor fan housing
10 Gun balance torsion arm
11 Torsion bar
12 MG belt bag stowage
13 Co-axial MG with belt bags in place
14 5cm L/60 gun breech
15 Elevating handwheel
16 Traverse indicator
17 Sighting telescope
18 Voice tubes, commander/gunner

7 RTR; they lost several vehicles and were bundled back the way they had come.

At dawn on the morning of 15 May Halfaya Pass fell to a *coup de main* carried out by 'C' Squadron, 4 RTR, another Matilda regiment. Rommel was adamant that the Pass should be retaken, and on 27 May no less than 160 tanks, organized in three battlegroups and led by PzKpfw IIIs, converged towards its head. An incredible sight met the eyes of their commanders; nine Matildas, all that 'C' Squadron could muster, were crawling out to meet them, covering the withdrawal of their infantry down onto the coastal plain. Eagerly the German gunners set their sights and loosed off round after round, only to see the 37mm and 50mm shot go flying off the Matildas' thick hides. Unlike the Char B, the Matilda did not have vulnerable radiator louvres, and its tracks were better protected; in addition, the drill in its three-man turret was every bit as efficient as that in the PzKpfw III, and the return fire of the 2pdrs. could penetrate the armour of every German and Italian vehicle present at the normal battle range of 500 to 800 yards. German tanks in the leading ranks of the *keil* began to explode and burn without any apparent reduction in the enemy's strength. Those behind, even less capable of engaging on even terms, started a retrogressive movement which soon took an entire battalion out of range. Satisfied, the three surviving Matildas retired down the Pass, picking up the crews of the six which had been immobilized by track damage.

Such an event was unparalleled in the history of the *Panzerwaffe*, and Rommel was beside himself with rage at the propaganda victory handed to the British. The unfortunate battalion commander was court-martialled, his immediate superior dismissed out of hand, and the commander of 5th Light Division removed from his post. That there existed among Panzer crews a very real fear of the Matilda was quite understandable, for the only effective defence at the time was the 88mm anti-aircraft gun firing in the anti-tank rôle. However, '88s' were only to be had at a premium, and an immediate request was made for Panzerjäger to be despatched to Africa to restore the balance.

In June the British mounted their first major offensive to relieve Tobruk, Operation 'Battleaxe', capturing Fort Capuzzo on the 15th. At first light the following day 15th Panzer Division launched a counter-attack, but drove into an ambush laid by 'A' and 'B' Squadrons, 7 RTR. Fifty of the division's 80 fighting vehicles were lost before it was able to extricate itself. The divisional commander, mindful of the fate of his colleagues following the Halfaya débâcle, quickly regrouped and by-passed Capuzzo, hoping to isolate it from the east; his only reward was to be stalled yet again by Matildas, this time manned by 'B' Squadron, 4 RTR, at a ridge known as Point 206.

Farther south, 5th Light Division was fighting a successful offensive/defensive battle against the Cruisers of 7th Armoured Brigade whose two regiments (2 and 6 RTR) had blunted their potential against an anti-tank gun screen at Hafid Ridge. 5th Light's Panzers had then sallied forth to engage the 'Desert Rats' in a running fight during which 6 RTR's new Crusader tanks broke down at an alarming rate. The German intention was to sweep north to the coast, thus trapping the British troops in the Capuzzo area; but before this could be achieved 'Battleaxe' was

cancelled and an escape corridor held open by two Matilda squadrons, each of which held off an entire German division for a day.

During the tank battles the British had knocked out more than 100 German tanks, but only 12 of these were completely written off, the rest being recovered and repaired. Their own loss had been 91 vehicles, many of them simple breakdowns which could have been recovered had it not been for high-level muddle and misunderstanding. This time it was the heads of senior British officers which rolled.

It was not until November that a further attempt was made to relieve Tobruk. Operation 'Crusader' was a much larger affair than 'Battleaxe' and included three armoured brigades (4th, 7th and 22nd) as well as two tank brigades, the 1st covering the northern flank with XIII Corps, and the 32nd the Tobruk garrison's break-out. British first line tank strength was 756, that of the Axis 320.

But while Rommel fought with both his Panzer divisions concentrated (5th Light had been re-styled as 21st Panzer), the British armoured brigades each pursued their separate objectives, with the result that within days of the start of the offensive 7th Armoured Brigade was removed from the board while the 4th and 22nd were left confused and dispersed. However, Rommel's brief foray into Egypt by which he hoped, unsuccessfully, to destroy the British commander's nerve, provided just sufficient time for a reorganization to be carried out. Tobruk was relieved by XIII Corps, isolated again, and finally relieved for the last time while sheer attrition, both tactical and mechanical, reduced the German strength to such a dangerous level that Cyrenaica had to be evacuated. Some 300 Axis tanks had been destroyed as opposed to a British loss of 187. In addition to the casualties sustained by the Panzer divisions in actions with the British armour, other causes of loss included breakdowns induced by the PzKpfw III's inefficient air filters, and tanks destroyed by 2pdr. *portees* and 25pdrs. firing over open sights, a reminder that the British did not hold a monopoly in charging unshaken gun-lines (see Vanguard 10, *Allied Tank Destroyers*).

Rommel's remarkable resilience was demonstrated in January 1942 when, having received a meagre reinforcement of tanks, he riposted so

Interesting view of an abandoned German field workshop in Tunisia, spring 1943. (Martin Windrow)

unexpectedly that much of the lost ground was recovered, the line eventually being stabilized at Gazala. Here both sides began to build up their strength for the next round. *Panzerarmee Afrika* eventually accumulated 228 Italian tanks, 50 PzKpfw IIs, 40 75mm howitzer PzKpfw IVs, 223 L/42 50mm PzKpfw IIIs and 19 L/60 50mm PzKpfw IIIs, a total of 560 tanks. Opposing them would be 843 British tanks, of which the most significant were the 167 Grants, new arrivals in the desert, which, with their sponson-mounted 75mm guns put the British ahead for once in tank-killing potential.

The Axis got in the first and vital blow on 27 May. The Grants tore great holes in the ranks of the Panzer divisions (see Vanguard 6, *The Lee/Grant Tanks in British Service*); but the British fought in the same unco-ordinated fashion they had employed during 'Crusader', missed priceless opportunities, and ultimately suffered a disastrous defeat which cost them most of their armour and which was followed almost immediately by the surrender of Tobruk. It was the PzKpfw III's crowning achievement in Africa,

and earned Rommel his Field Marshal's baton.

The *Afrika Korps* had also suffered severely, and the pursuit of the beaten 8th Army was carried out with a mere handful of tanks. These succeeded in turning the British out of their defensive position at Mersa Matruh, but lacked the necessary 'clout' to penetrate the newly forming line at El Alamein.

By the end of August Rommel had been reinforced sufficiently to attempt a repeat of the right hook with which he had begun the Gazala/Knightsbridge battle. In addition to 243 Italian M13s, he had 71 L/60 and 93 L/42 PzKpfw IIIs, 10 of the older PzKpfw IVs and a handful of light tanks; of greater significance was the arrival of 27 PzKpfw IVF2s, armed with an L/43 75mm gun, which would become his cutting edge—a clear indication that the PzKpfw III was now falling below battlefield requirements. In the event, the offensive was severely checked at Alam Halfa ridge and the Axis army thrown onto the defensive by an acute shortage of fuel.

This was a factor which the 8th Army's new commander, Lt.-Gen. Bernard Montgomery, intended to exploit to the full in the planning for the Second Battle of Alamein. 8th Army would fight a 'crumbling' battle, attacking first in one place and then another, forcing the Panzer divisions to burn irreplaceable petrol driving between sectors in the counter-attack rôle. It was a strategy against which Rommel had no effective defence, since a breakthrough would spell annihilation for his army.

When the battle began on 23 October 8th Army could deploy over 1,000 tanks, including 170 Grants and 252 Shermans, with more in reserve. Axis tank strength was 278 M13s, 85 L/42 and 88 L/60 PzKpfw IIIs, eight old PzKpfw IVs and 30 PzKpfw IVF2s. During major tank engagements such as Tel el Aqqaqir the British lost the greater number of vehicles, but Rommel's strength was effectively whittled away until defeat became inevitable. By the time the battle ended the Italian armoured divisions had ceased to exist and all but a handful of German tanks had been destroyed or abandoned on the battlefield, while the *Afrika Korps* began its long withdrawal to Tunisia.

Most of the subsequent fighting took place in mountainous country. With the Anglo-American 1st Army closing in on their last African bridgehead the Germans hastily shipped over the 10th Panzer Division, sufficient tanks to re-equip 15th and 21st Panzer Divisions, and a Tiger battalion. A notable success was gained against the US 1st Armored Division at Kasserine Pass, but the end could not be long delayed, and on 12 May 1943 the war in Africa was officially over. (See Vanguard 10, *Allied Tank Destroyers*, and Vanguard 13, *The Churchill Tank*.)

During the final phase the PzKpfw III remained the most numerous tank in the German order of battle, but an increasing number of those reaching the front were the 75mm-armed Ausf. N. 'The reasons why the 75mm short gun was gaining favour at the expense of the long 50mm gun seem to have been mainly two. The nature of the fighting tipped the balance towards HE rather than armour-piercing shell, while the introduction of hollow-charge ammunition for the 75mm gun in the summer of 1942 improved its all-round usefulness.'*

*The British official history of the campaign, *The Mediterranean and Middle East*, Vol IV, page 500, Major-General I. S. O. Playfair and others.

Organization of Panzer Division, 1941

Organization was by no means standard, but note general trends. Infantry-to-tank ratio increased since 1940. Motorcycle Bn. from Mechanized Inf. Bde. sometimes merged with Div. Recce Bn., and in due course disappeared altogether. Mechanized Inf. known as Rifle Regts. until 1942, Panzer-Grenadiers thereafter.

Russia

No one really knows how many tanks the Soviet Union possessed in 1941, but the lowest estimate places the figure at not less than 20,000. They varied from multi-turreted dinosaurs like the T-100, T-35 and T-28 to the small amphibious T-37 tankettes. By Western standards they were crudely finished, but they were robust and intentionally simple in layout, since their crews were drawn from an as-yet technically unsophisticated population.

For many years the Russians had followed the French theory of infantry support, leading the attack with heavy tanks and following up with T-26s accompanying the foot-soldiers, while exploitation formations equipped with the fast BT Series stood by ready to exploit the breakthrough. However, the success of the German *blitzkrieg* tactics in Poland and France, together with their own shortcomings in Spain and Finland, had led Red Army commanders to appreciate the flaws in their doctrine and to design formations which bore some resemblance to the

Newly arrived Ausf. N in Tunisia, 1943. Two-digit turret numbers usually indicated the platoon and the individual tank; '04' is probably a battalion headquarters vehicle, and bears the sign of 15th Panzer Division—see Plate B and commentary. (Bundesarchiv)

Panzer divisions. It was unfortunate that the basic structure of the Soviet armoured corps was in this transitional stage when Hitler launched his invasion.

This was bad enough, but in addition Russian tactical response was infinitely slower even than the French. A totalitarian, ruthlessly centralized state required absolute obedience rather than initiative from all but its most senior officers, and since the officer corps had been mercilessly purged of progressive elements during the 1930s, the safest course for an individual was to wait for orders from above. This was hardly an ideal situation in which to enter a battle the tempo of which would be dictated by Panzer commanders who made their decisions among their leading vehicles and whose goal was continuous mobility. To compound a thoroughly unsatisfactory state

29

Close-up of an Ausf. N, almost certainly of the same sub-unit as that in the previous photograph. The colour scheme appears to be the darker yellow used on some German tanks in the last stages of the African fighting. (Martin Windrow)

of affairs, Russian armoured units lacked tactical flexibility since the issue of radios extended downwards only as far as battalion commanders, so that orders on the move could only be transmitted between vehicles by flag or hand signal.

On the other hand, the Russians had some brilliant designers who were particularly skilled in producing vehicles with a sound gun/armour relationship. The new KV heavy and the T-34 medium tanks both carried a 76.2mm gun which was better than anything the *Panzerwaffe* possessed, while the KV's armour was comparable to the British Matilda's; the T-34's angled plate was almost as good, and its Christie suspension gave running speeds well in excess of those of the German battle tanks (see Vanguard 14, *The T-34 Tank*).

Hitler had long sought a confrontation with Bolshevik Russia, and his offensive would have been launched in the spring of 1941 had he not

been forced to secure his right flank by invading Yugoslavia and rescuing Mussolini's armies from their hopeless involvement with the Greeks. These short campaigns had demonstrated once again the decisive teamwork between the Luftwaffe and the Panzer divisions, and were notable for the determination of the German tank crews to force their machines through some of the most difficult country in Europe; they also absorbed valuable time which would have to be subtracted from the operational period available before the onset of the Russian winter.

The onslaught on Russia, Operation 'Barbarossa', began on 22 June 1941. Germany had available 3,200 tanks, of which 1,440 were PzKpfw IIIs and 517 PzKpfw IVs; a total of 17 armoured divisions, organized in four *Panzergruppen*, took part in the initial assault. The forward units of the Red Air Force were destroyed on the ground and the tank spearheads began to roll forward. When encountered, resistance was fierce but uncoordinated. German operators monitoring the radio frequencies of higher Russian formations heard time and again the plaintive request,

'What are we to do? We must have orders!' But few men had the courage to make decisions without consulting higher authority, and those who did found that by the time their orders reached the troops, the tactical situation was radically different from that in which they had been conceived. Repeatedly the *Panzergruppen* wheeled together to form huge pockets which were reduced by the follow-up infantry divisions, yielding vast numbers of prisoners and enormous quantities of equipment. In Moscow, Stalin reacted in characteristic Soviet fashion by demanding a scapegoat, and shot his leading tank expert—a step which failed to bring about any radical improvement in the Red Army's position.

It was a staggering débâcle, which ultimately cost the Red Army 1,000,000 men, and 17,000 tanks knocked out, captured or simply abandoned by their crews after they had broken down. In a little over three weeks one Panzer group alone advanced 400 miles; and it seemed as though Moscow, hub of the all-important Russian railway system, was there for the taking.

But other factors were also at work. In France the Panzer divisions had been set an objective that was mechanically attainable, the Channel; in Russia the objectives were so far distant that the German heavy repair system simply could not cope with the numbers of breakdowns, which increased with every mile covered. Again, battle casualties had been higher than in previous campaigns, accounting for 2,700 vehicles, so that after ten weeks' fighting the Panzer spearheads had been reduced to mere shadows of their former selves.

Whether Moscow could have been taken before the deteriorating weather brought all movement to a standstill remains an open question, but Hitler's meddling with the dispositions of the *Panzergruppen* certainly provided the Red Army with an unexpected bonus in time. Russia survived, and her limitless potential would ensure that the scales would tilt slowly but irrevocably against Nazi Germany.

When tank had met tank, the PzKpfw IIIs had dealt easily with the elderly T-35s, the T-26s and the thin-skinned BTs; but the KV provided an unpleasant surprise. Squatting on a causeway, a

Nice study of PzKpfw III Ausf. Js of 24th Panzer Division moving into a forward zone during the 1942 Russian campaign. This formation favoured large rear stowage boxes, on which were marked the divisional sign, commemorating its origins in the old *1. Kavallerie-Division*—see Plate C. The 24th Panzer was lost at Stalingrad, but re-formed several months later. (Bundesarchiv)

single KV could hold up an entire Panzer division for a day, shrugging off rounds from every gun that could be brought to bear, and in such circumstances the only effective answer was for German infantry to stalk the brute with explosive charges. The 37mm gun was useless against these monsters, and although the L/42 50mm could score a kill this was usually achieved at a range of 50 yards or less, and preferably from the rear. The superb T-34 was an even greater headache for Panzer crews who sincerely believed at the start of the campaign that they held a wide lead in technology over their Russian counterparts, and as far as the PzKpfw III was concerned not even the fitting of the L/60 gun could bridge the gap; the balance was redressed, bloodily, by inept Russian tactics opposed to German expertise and initiative.

For the Wehrmacht, the major event of 1942 was the great drive into the Caucasus in pursuit of the Baku oilfields. Once more the tank columns motored across the steppe under cloudless skies, and as the miles disappeared beneath their tracks it seemed as though the Panzer divisions were to enjoy a second 'Happy Time'. There was,

in fact, very little fighting, for the Red Army had learned its lesson and had side-stepped the principal thrust.

But on the eastern flank of the advance lay Stalingrad, concerning which Hitler developed a total megalomania. All available reserves were diverted to the capture of the city, a fact duly noted by the Russian Supreme Command (*Stavka*), which responded with a gigantic double envelopment, trapping the German 6th Army, and part of 4th Panzer Army as well, which had been forced against its better judgement to take part in the street-fighting. The bitter struggle continued until 2 February 1943, when the newly created Field Marshal von Paulus surrendered with 200,000 of his men.

Stalingrad had been a disaster which not only shook the German Army to its core, but which also opened the door on the even more horrendous possibility of the Red Army encircling those forces now hastily withdrawing from the Caucasus; all that was needed was a determined thrust south-west to the Sea of Azov, and their fate would be sealed.

Stavka detailed two armies for the task, Vatutin's South-West Front and Golikov's Voronezh Front, and for a while they had a free run. This was permitted as a matter of deliberate policy by von Manstein, the Commander-in-Chief of Army

Ausf. N in southern Russia, winter 1942/43. The vehicle's mint condition implies recent delivery; and the symbol on the hull side, well forward, may possibly be a stylized outline of Panzer Regiment 31's famous red devil insignia. (Bundesarchiv)

PzKpfw III Ausf. Ls of 3rd SS Panzer Division 'Totenkopf' moving up for the attack on the Kursk Salient, July 1943: the division formed part of 1st SS Panzer Korps, which played a major rôle in the great tank battle of Prokhorovka. To the right of the temporary divisional sign is the cover for the inertia starter port. See Plate E and commentary. (Bundes-archiv)

Group South, who was fully aware of Soviet intentions. He appreciated that because of Russian inexperience in deep-penetration operations and poor logistic back-up, both Soviet armies would quickly outrun their supply echelons and that the inevitable breakdowns would steadily drain away the strength of their tank formations; conversely, he did not wish to launch his own counter-offensive until the German armour had been sufficiently concentrated for a knock-out blow, for Stalingrad had cost the Army 800 Panzers and the average strength of his Panzer divisions was now 27 tanks.

On 20 February 1943 he moved at last, slicing into Vatutin's flank and finding most of the Russian columns stalled for want of fuel. South-West Front was routed and forced into a precipitate retreat, losing 615 tanks, 400 guns, 23,000 men killed and 9,000 captured. Golikov, hastening to his stricken comrade's aid, was caught while still deploying and handled even more severely. Voronezh Front was thrown back across the Donets, leaving behind 600 tanks, 500 guns and 40,000 casualties. Only the *rasputitsa*,

the great thaw which turned hard-frozen ground into impassable mud, brought an end to Manstein's runaway progress.

This operation completely restored the integrity of the Eastern Front, and was the last occasion on which the PzKpfw III played the major rôle in a successful strategic offensive; indeed, it was the *Panzerwaffe*'s strategic success of the war, for in July its potential was irrevocably blunted against the interminable defensive belts of the Kursk salient, and then written down in the great tank battle of Prokhorovka, the largest of the Second World War, in which machines rammed each other or fought murderous duels at point-blank range. Kursk cost the Germans 1,500 tanks, which could not be spared, and the Russians about the same, which were replaced almost at once from factories safe beyond the Urals.

Thereafter, the PzKpfw III soldiered on in decreasing numbers, its place as the Panzer divisions' main battle tank being taken by the PzKpfw IV and the Panther, its last actions being fought during the great defensive battles of 1944.

*　*　*

Technically the PzKpfw III was, despite minor faults, a well-balanced basic design which left provision for up-gunning and up-armouring, but by 1942 it was incapable of further modification that would enable it to keep pace with the spiral of the gun/armour race. During the high years of *blitzkrieg* it was the only weapon in the German tank arsenal that really counted and thus, like Napoleon's *vieux moustaches*, it did not merely witness history in the making—it made it, from the Channel to the Volga and from the Arctic to the North African desert. This achievement has, perhaps, been overshadowed in recent years by the study of later and more dramatic German designs, but the fact remains that it was the PzKpfw III that brought Hitler closest to achieving his wildest dreams.

The PzKpfw III

BASIC TECHNICAL DETAILS

Ausf. F

Weight:	20 tons (Ausf. M: 20.8 tons)
Crew:	5
Armament:	1 × KwK L/42 50mm gun (Ausf. M: 1 × KwK 39 L/60 50mm gun) 2 × 7.92mm machine guns
Armour:	30mm (Ausf. M: 30mm plus 20mm or 30mm)
Engine:	Maybach HL 120 TRM, 300hp
Speed:	25mph
Overall length:	17ft. 9in. (Ausf. M: 21ft. 6in.)
Width:	9ft. 7in. (Ausf. M: 9ft. 9in.)
Height:	8ft. 3in.

The Plates

A1: PzKpfw III Ausf. A, 2.Panzer-Division, Poland, 1939
The overall colour scheme is standard 'Panzer grey', with the large white '223' on the turret side identifying company, *zug* and vehicle respectively. During this campaign Polish anti-tank gunners took a far heavier toll of the Panzers than was realized by the rest of the world, and the plain white German national cross used at first was soon considered to be far too conspicuous. A normal practice was to paint it over in yellow, sometimes—as here—leaving a thin white border. The division's first tactical sign, two yellow dots, appears over the inner side of the driver's visor. The operations of this division took them through an area cut by numerous small streams, and this crew have acquired a rough fascine of pine logs to ease their passage.

A2: PzKpfw III Ausf. E, 2.Panzer-Division, Balkans, 1941
Panzer Regiment 3, the tank component of this formation, abandoned large turret numbers and marked smaller on the forward side-plates of the hull. For internal recognition purposes coloured geometric symbols were painted on the turret sides—in the case of the 4th Company, an open red triangle on a yellow square. Another peculiarity of this company, at least, was the fixing of a polished horseshoe in a prominent position on the offside track-guard. Note the divisional sign, now one of the combinations of Y-rune and bars used by most formations, left of the driver's visor. The white stripe under it is unexplained.

A3: PzKpfw III Ausf. J, 14.Panzer-Division, Russia, 1941
The all-grey scheme is enlivened by the rarely seen white Panzer rhombus marking on the turret sides and rear bin, beneath the vehicle number '14'. These markings are repeated on the spare turret bin lying on the engine deck. The 'K' probably indicates a company commander's vehicle. White outline crosses of the type standard for this period appear on the hull side and rear, and an air recognition flag is draped over the turret roof. The yellow divisional sign, similar to an

Odalrune, is marked on the offside of the rear hull plate.

B1: PzKpfw III Ausf. G, DAK, Libya, 1941

There is a definite 'early days' look about this Ausf. G; the original Panzer grey is starting to show through the hastily applied sand-yellow 'slap'. The turret carries the number '612' in red trimmed with white, and the *Afrika Korps* palm and swastika are marked small on the hull side beneath the turret door forward hinge line. A large air recognition flag is lashed over the stowage on the rear deck; and the addition of road wheels and tracks to the front armour testify to an awareness of the 'Matilda menace'. A meticulous gunner has manufactured his own canvas muzzle cover and mounting sleeve, to protect his 'baby' as far as possible from the dust. The slung sun-helmets suggest a recently arrived crew — most old hands threw these over the side, as being about the most useless headgear for a tank-man that could be conceived.

B2: PzKpfw III Ausf. J, ex-21.Panzer-Division, North Africa, 1942

The history of this pale sand-yellow Ausf. J can be read in its markings. In the centre of the front plate is 21.Panzer-Division's tactical sign in

An unidentified PzKpfw III battalion passes a ruined village in the Mius-Stalino area, August 1943. The lead vehicle has a turret-girdle of spaced armour but appears to carry side-skirts on the far side only. (Bundesarchiv)

white; the turret carries the white outline numbers '111' indicating that the original owners were 1st Company, Panzer Regiment 22. It then seems to have enjoyed a spell in British service, perhaps after abandonment due to a breakdown; for on the offside front is the rhinoceros sign of 1st Armoured Division, and on the nearside the tactical number 86, indicating 9th Lancers. That some attempt was made to take the tank into regimental service is attested by the 'B' Squadron square painted on the turret; but this attempt was undoubtedly stamped upon, and the vehicle was sent back for evaluation, acquiring the evaluation number 'A100' in the process.

B3: PzKpfw III Ausf. N, 15.Panzer-Division, Tunisia, 1942–43

The track links draped over the turret roof of this Ausf. N. reflect the growing Allied air superiority of this period; additional track links and sandbags are also fitted to the front of the hull. As yet this tank seems to have seen little wear and tear, and the dark mustard shade favoured (along with olive green) for German armour in Tunisia is still intact. The turret numbers are '04', in black

35

outlined with white; the national cross on the hull side is also black and white. The divisional sign is painted beside the driver's visor in the red usually employed by this division. It is interesting that this vehicle lacks the three smoke dischargers normally mounted on each turret side of this Mark—a photograph in this book shows them fitted to the next tank in this troop.

C1: PzKpfw III Ausf. H, 10.Panzer-Division, Russia, 1941–42

The national cross, in white outline, is painted on a supplementary bin which has been welded to the track-guard; behind this, the vehicle serial number '621' is painted on a black rhomboid plate, a system favoured in the immediate pre-war years. The tank's precise place in the regi-

mental order of battle is not revealed by the single number '5', in red outlined white, on the turret side; to the rear of this is the white-sprayed outline of Panzer Regiment 7's bison badge. The yellow divisional sign is visible beside the driver's side visor.

C2: PzKpfw III Ausf. J, 24.Panzer-Division, Russia, 1942

In common with many tanks of this division photographed in Russia, this L/60 Ausf. J has a large stowage bin fixed across the rear of the engine deck, and on this can be seen the black and white national cross and the division's distinctive sign. A log has been lashed below the bin, doubtless as an unditching beam. The turret number '525' in red, outlined white, identifies the 2nd *Zug*, 5th Company. The origins of this formation, raised from the old 1.Kavallerie-Division, are recalled in the yellow uniform piping which contrasted with the rose-coloured *Waffenfarbe* of the rest of the Army tank units.

**D1: PzKpfw III Ausf. M, thought to be of
3.SS-Panzer-Division 'Totenkopf', Kursk, 1943**
The new standard overall colour scheme of dark
yellow, with added camouflage in the form of
red-brown blotches, covers even the spare track
links on the tank's nose and the large wooden
stowage crate on the rear deck. The forward
plate of the hull skirt armour is missing, but the
turret-girdle is intact, and bears the tank number
'421' in plain black.

**D2: PzKpfw III Ausf. J, 1.SS-Panzer-Division
'Leibstandarte Adolf Hitler', Russia, 1943**
Photographed, possibly near Belgorod, towards
the end of von Manstein's 1943 offensive, this
tank still wears basic Panzer grey, but has been
heavily overpainted with white snow camouflage.
The rear face of the turret bin has been left grey as
a background to the white-outline tank number

'555', which has been roughly repainted in red on
the turret sides. Grey areas have also been left
around the national cross on the hull side, and
the divisional sign on the nearside of the rear
hull plate. The national cross is repeated beside
this.

**E1: PzKpfw III Ausf. M command tank, unidentified
artillery unit, Russia, 1943–44**
By this stage of the war the PzKpfw III was of
little use as a main battle tank, but numbers
served on as headquarters vehicles with heavy
tank destroyer battalions—a position hinted at
by the turret number '001'. The overall dark
yellow colour scheme has been sprayed with
streaks of red-brown and dark green; the forward
plate of the rather hard-worn skirt armour is
evidently a replacement. The tank's outline is

37

partly broken up by the addition of birch saplings—we have 'thinned out' this foliage for clarity. The national cross on the turret girdle is unusual in that the centre is in the yellow ground-colour, inside a thin black cross outlined with white. At the front bottom corner of the girdle is the name 'Brigitte' in white Gothic script. The commander wears artillery uniform.

E2: PzKpfw III Ausf. L, 3.SS-Panzer-Division 'Totenkopf', Kursk, July 1943

Note the large strap-iron stowage rack welded across the rear hull; these were common, and as they were strictly a unit modification they took many varying forms. The tank number '823' is roughly painted on the rear of the turret bin, without white trim. On the nearside of the rear hull plate is the three-pronged temporary divisional sign adopted for the Kursk offensive, Operation 'Zitadelle'. Another variant of the national cross appears on the offside, this one a 'Luftwaffe' style of thin proportions, black outlined with white with a black outer trim.

F (top): Driving compartment interior, PzKpfw III Ausf. J

See numbered key on page 25. The photographs from which this painting has been prepared show a manufacturer's serial '6900?', identifying an Ausf. J. Here we see the gearbox and instrument panel on the right; the driver's controls, vision devices and final drive housing ahead. The seat back has been removed for clarity.

F (bottom): Radio operator/hull gunner's position, PzKpfw III Ausf. J

See numbered key on page 25. The receiver is mounted left, on the transmission housing, and the transmitter ahead of the seat, with a folding table for message pads, etc. To the right is the hull machine gun, linked to the elevating cap immediately above the seat.

G (top): Commander's position, PzKpfw III Ausf. J

See numbered key on page 25. The commander's seat, mounted on the turret ring, is seen as if looking backwards and up from under the breech of the L/42 gun. Part of the gunner's seat can be seen on the right, and the recoil shield above, with the counterweight ingot set into the rear of the spent-case deflector shield.

G (bottom): Turret interior, PzKpfw III Ausf. J

See numbered key on page 25. This is an L/60 model—note torsion bar counter-balance mechanism. Near this can be seen the extractor fan cage, and the internal main armament travelling crutch. To the left can be seen the two ends of the commander's/gunner's flexible voice tube, part of the elevating handwheel, the sighting telescope, and a rudimentary 'clock' traverse indicator.

H1: Private, Army Panzertruppen, 1939–40

The two-piece padded beret bears national insignia in white thread, and the national eagle also appears on the right breast of the double-breasted black 'crossover' tunic. The shirt is 'mouse grey', the tie black. The tunic is piped round the upper lapel and collar in the rose Waffenfarbe of this arm of service; the patches on the collar, piped in rose and bearing white metal death's-heads, were common to all ranks of the Panzerwaffe up to and frequently including general officers. The similarly piped shoulder-straps, sewn down to prevent snagging in the vehicle, are of the plain design worn by all ranks up to Unteroffizier. He holds a round of 37mm High Explosive with a trace in the base of the projectile, this being indicated by the silver-painted head and yellow band.

H2: Panzer crewman, Russia, summer 1941

The shoulder-straps from the black tunic are worn here on the shirt—these were the only authorized insignia for the shirt. The black Army-pattern sidecap of 1940 issue has the national eagle in less visible pale grey thread on black backing, and the national cockade is enclosed by a V of rose piping. He holds a round of Armour-Piercing Capped ammunition for the 'short' L/42 50mm gun.

H3: Panzer crewman, Deutsches Afrika Korps, 1942

The tropical version of the sidecap, in Olive Drab lined with red cloth, was often much faded, and it was fashionable to deliberately bleach them with anti-gas capsules, so that a pale sandy shade was quite common. Insignia are embroidered on a tan ground, the national eagle being in pale blue-grey thread. The usual V of rose *Waffenfarbe* is worn. The shirt is similarly bleached, and bears the olive cloth shoulder-straps from the tropical uniform, piped rose, with an olive-painted button. The white metal identity disc bore the man's particulars on each side of the central perforations. He has evidently just cleared the turret of hot spent cases, hence the gloves; he holds an Armour-Piercing AP.40 round for the 'short' 50mm L/42.

H4: Panzer crewman, 3.SS-Panzer-Division 'Totenkopf', 1942–43

The black sidecap, bearing Waffen-SS national eagle and SS death's-head badges in silver-grey thread, is of the distinctive cut used by the SS and Luftwaffe formations. It is tied on his head with a scarf, against the bitter Russian winter; and he also wears the black Panzer jacket buttoned across and closed to the throat. The front join of the SS pattern was vertical, rather than slanted

Ausf. M with skirt armour and turret girdle, by-passing a culvert which engineers are constructing across a stream for wheeled transport. Comparison with other photographs gives a probable identification of *3. SS-Panzer-Division 'Totenkopf'* on its way to take part in the Kursk 'death ride', July 1943. See Plate D. (Bundesarchiv)

in the Army manner. The collar is not piped, and bears two identical silver-grey thread death's-head devices. This was peculiar to this formation, whose insignia was the death's-head; normally Waffen-SS privates wore divisional insignia on the right collar only, and a blank black patch on the left. The SS-pattern national eagle appears on the upper left sleeve, and the divisional cuff-title on the same forearm. The rose of the armoured troops appears only as piping on the shoulder-straps and in a V on the cap front. He holds a round of High Explosive ammunition for the 'long' L/60 50mm gun.

Notes sur les planches en couleur

A1 La croix nationale blanche qui était peinte sur les chars au début de la campagne polonaise était trop visible et était donc souvent repeinte en jaune. Les troncs de bois sont une fascine pour faciliter la traversée des rivières. **A2** Le triangle rouge sur carré jaune semble être un insigne de compagnie ou de peloton, un système particulier à ce régiment. D'autres chars de la 4ème compagnie, qui ont été photographiés, portaient également le fer à cheval illustré ici. **A3** Le losange blanc était rarement vu après le déclenchement de la guerre. Notez le drapeau national peint sur le toit de la tourelle pour faciliter la reconnaissance aérienne; le coffre supplémentaire sur le blindage arrière; et la marque 'K' qui indique probablement qu'il s'agit du char d'un commandant.

B1 La peinture originale grise est visible à travers la couche de peinture jaune sable appliquée hâtivement par dessus. Numéro de tourelle '612'; notez le petit insigne de l'Afrika Korps sur le côté de la coque. **B2** Les marques indiquent que ce char servait autrefois avec la 21ème Panzer Division (voir l'insigne au milieu de l'avant de la coque) avec le 1er peloton, 1ère compagnie du Panzer Regt. 22 ('111' sur la tourelle). Après avoir été capturé, il a été utilisé par le 'B' Sqn. (insigne carré sur la tourelle), 9th Lancers ('86' sur l'avant de la coque, à droite) 1st Armoured Division britannique (insigne d'un rhinocéros sur l'avant de la coque, à gauche) avant d'être renvoyé à l'arrière pour un examen technique ('A100' est le numéro d'un dépôt d'examen). **B3** La couleur moutarde foncée était utilisée, avec du vert olive, pour les chars allemands en Tunisie. Des patins de chenilles de rechange et des sacs remplis de sable servaient de protection supplémentaire. L'emblème de cette division était normalement peint en rouge.

C1 Cette manière de porter le numéro de série du véhicule sur un losange appliqué sur le côté de la coque date d'avant la guerre. Le numéro sur la tourelle est réduit à un seul chiffre '5', derrière lequel est visible l'insigne du bison du Panzer Regt. 7: l'emblème de la division est à côté de la plaque de vision du pilote. **C2** Le grand coffre supplémentaire posé sur le blindage arrière porte l'insigne national et l'emblème de la division; le galon jaune sur l'uniforme du commandant rappelle les origines cavalières de cette division.

D1 En 1943 le schéma de couleurs normal a été changé de gris en jaune foncé; les équipages y ajoutaient un camouflage de peinture marron et/ou verte. Sur ce char SS la peinture de camouflage couvre même la chenille de rechange sur l'avant de la coque et la caisse en bois sur le pontage arrière. **D2** La surface arrière du coffre sur la tourelle, peinte en gris, a été laissée telle quelle sur ce char, dont le reste est peint en blanc pour le camoufler dans la neige, et ceci pour révéler les numéros du char, qui sont également grossièrement repeints en rouge sur le côté de la tourelle. Notez l'emblème de la division et les emblèmes nationaux sur fond gris non camouflé.

E1 Ceci est probablement un char de commande dans un bataillon anti-chars blindé—notez les antennes supplémentaires et le numéro '001'. Notez également la manière inhabituelle de peindre la croix sur la tourelle et le prénom 'Brigitte' sur le blindage de la tourelle. **E2** Notez l'emblème divisionnaire spécial, adopté temporairement pour l'offensive de Kursk, sur l'arrière de la coque, à gauche, et le porte-bagages typique, soudé à l'arrière de la coque.

F (en haut) Poste du pilote, face à la route; voir la légende en langue anglaise à la page 25. Le tableau de bord et le levier de vitesse sont visibles à droite; levier de commande et appareils de vue, au milieu; gyrocompas, dispositif de vision latérale, sacs de munitions pour la mitrailleuse supplémentaire, masque à gaz, à gauche. **F (en bas)** Poste de l'opérateur de T.S.F./tireur. Poste de radio à gauche: poste émetteur, avec une petite table pliante pour les blocs-notes, etc., devant le siège. La mitrailleuse a un 'bonnet' en caoutchouc sur un bras métallique, dans lequel le tireur met sa tête pour contrôler l'élévation, car il avait besoin de ses deux mains pour tirer et pour introduire la bande-chargeur.

G (en haut) Siège du chef de char et coupole, en regardant vers le haut et vers l'arrière d'en dessous de la culasse du canon. La siège est monté sur la roue de la tourelle et il y a de la place autour de lui pour ranger de petits articles d'équipement. Le poids encastré dans le déflecteur des obus brûlés indique que ce PzKpfw III J est équipé du canon L/42. **G (en bas)** Le balancier qui relie la culasse au toit indique que ce char est équipé du canon long L/60. Notez les tuyaux acoustiques reliant le chef de char au tireur, à gauche.

H1 L'uniforme des équipages de char entre 1939 et 1940, avec le béret en deux-pièces, matelassé et plutôt disgracieux. Les insignes sont brodés en fil blanc. L'obus du type à haut explosif pour le canon de 37mm. **H2** Le calot noir a remplacé le béret entre 1940 et 1941. L'obus est du type perforant pour le canon L/42 de 50mm. **H3** La version tropicale du calot était fabriquée en tissu vert olive, mais il était souvent décoloré. L'obus est du type 'AP.40' perforant pour le canon L/42 de 50mm. **H4** Style SS de l'uniforme de char conçu pour temps froid. L'usage par les soldats des emblèmes divisionnaires sur les deux insignes de col était particulier à la Division 'Totenkopf'. L'obus est du type à haut explosif pour le canon L/60 de 50mm.

Farbtafeln

A1 Das zu Beginn des Polenfeldzugs auf die Panzer aufgemalte weiße Nationalkreuz war zu auffällig und wurde häufig mit Gelb übermalt. Die Holzstämme dienten als Faschine zum Überqueren von Wasserläufen. **A2** Das rote Dreieck auf gelbem Quadrat ist wahrscheinlich ein Kompanie- oder Zugabzeichen, ein für dieses Regiment typisches Kennzeichnungssystem. Andere photographierte Panzer der 4. Kompanie trugen auch ein Hufeisen, wie hier gezeigt. **A3** Nach Ausbruch des Krieges war die weiße Raute als Markierung nur noch selten zu sehen. Man beachte die Nationalflagge auf dem Turmlukendeckel, die der Erkennung aus der Luft diente, den Reserve-Staubehälter auf dem hinteren Deck und die Markierung 'K', die vermutlich den Kommandeurspanzer einer Kompanie kennzeichnete.

B1 Die graue Originalfarbe scheint durch den hastig aufgebrachten sandgelben Anstrich durch. Turmnummer '612'; an der Panzerkörperseite ist das kleinformatige Kennzeichen des Afrika Korps zu sehen. **B2** Aus den Kennzeichen geht hervor, daß dieser Panzer in der 21. Panzerdivision (Abzeichen in der Mitte der vorderen Wannenpanzerung) im 1. Zug, 1. Kompanie des Panzer Regt. 22 ('111' am Turm) gedient hat. Als Beutepanzer wurde er von der 'B' Sqn. (rechteckiges Zeichen am Turm), 9th Lancers ('86' vorn rechts an der Wanne), britische 1st Armoured Division (Nashorn vorn links an der Wanne) eingesetzt, ehe er zur Überprüfung ('A100' ist eine Prüfungsdepot-Nummer) nach hinten geschickt wurde. **B3** In Tunesien wurde neben dem Olivgrün auch Dunkelbraun als Anstrich für die deutschen Panzer eingesetzt. Reservekettenlängen und Sandsäcke boten zusätzlichen Schutz. Das Emblem dieser Division war gewöhnlich in Rot.

C1 Die Fahrzeug-Seriennummer wird im Vor-Kriegs-Stil auf einer rautenförmigen Platte an der Panzerseite getragen. Die Turm-Nummer bestand aus einer Einzelzahl '5', hinter der das Büffel-Abzeichen des Panzer-Regt. 7 angebracht ist; das Divisionszeichen befindet sich neben dem Sehschlitz des Fahrers. **C2** Der große, nachträglich quer auf dem Panzerheck aufgesetzte Staukasten trägt das Hoheitsabzeichen und das Divisionszeichen; die gelbe Paspel an der Uniform des Panzerführers erinnert an den Kavallerie-Ursprung dieser Division.

D1 1943 wurde der Standard-Farbanstrich von Grau auf Dunkelgelb/Braungelb umgestellt; die Besatzungen fügten dann Tarnfarben in Braun und/oder Grün hinzu. Bei diesem SS-Panzer sind sogar die Reservekette an der Wannenfront und die Holzkiste auf dem Panzerheck von der Tarnfarbe erfaßt. **D2** Zur Kennzeichnung der Panzernummer ist die rückwärtige Fläche des Staukastens am Turm bei diesem für den Schnee getarnten Panzer grau geblieben; die Nummer ist auf der Turmseite grob in Rot aufgemalt. Auch das Divisions- und das Hoheitsabzeichen sind auf mit Tarnfarbe übermalten grauen Feldern aufgebracht.

E1 Vermutlich ein Befehlspanzer in einer schweren Panzerjäger-Abteilung—man beachte die zusätzlichen Antennen und die Zahl '001'. Interessant sind auch der ungewöhnliche Stil des Balkenkreuzes am Turm und der Name 'Brigitte' an der Turmpanzerung. **E2** Für die Kursk-Offensive wurde ein besonderes vorübergehendes Divisionsabzeichen, links am Panzerheck, übernommen; typisch ist auch die auf das Heck aufgeschweißte Stauvorrichtung.

F (oben) Fahrerposition, mit Blickrichtung nach vorn; siehe Erläuterungen in englischer Sprache auf S. 25. Auf der rechten Seite sind die Instrumententafel und der Schalthebel zu sehen; Lenkhebel und Sichtvorrichtungen in der Mitte; links befinden sich Kreiselkompaß, Seitensichtvorrichtung, Munitionstaschen und Gasmaske. **F (unten)** Funker-/MG-Schützenposition in der Panzerwanne. Funkempfänger links; Funkgerät mit kleinem Klapptisch für Meldezettel usw. vor dem Sitz. Das Maschinengewehr ist mit einer Gummikappe an einem Metallarm ausgestattet, in die der Schütze den Kopf drückte, um die Höhe des MGs zu richten—er brauchte beide Hände zum Schießen und Eingeben des Munitionsgurts.

G (oben) Sitz des Panzerkommandanten und *cupola*, Blickrichtung aufwärts nach hinten aus der Position unterhalb des Geschützverschlusses. Der Sitz ist am Turmkranz befestigt und von Stauräumen zum Unterbringen von kleinen Ausrüstungsgegenständen umgeben. Das Gewicht hinten am Hülsenabweisschild zeigt, daß dieser PzKpfw III J mit der früheren Kanone L/42 bestückt ist. **G (unten)** Der den Verschluß mit dem Deck verbindende Ausgleicharm zeigt, daß dieser Panzer das lange Geschütz L/60 aufweist. Die oben angebrachte Schiene wurde zum Herausheben des Munitionsblocks für Wartungszwecke verwendet. Auf der linken Seite sind die Sprachrohre für die Sprechverbindung zwischen Kommandeur und Schützen zu sehen.

H1 Die Uniform der Panzerbesatzungen 1939–40 mit dem uneleganten zweiteiligen, ausgestopften Barett. Die Abzeichen bestehen aus weißem Fadenmaterial. Bei der Granate handelt es sich um ein Panzersprenggeschoß für das 37-mm-Geschütz. **H2** Die schwarze Feldmütze löste 1940–41 das Barett ab. Die Granate ist ein 'panzerdurchschlagendes Haubengeschoß' für das 50-mm-Geschütz L/42. **H3** Die Tropenausführung der Feldmütze war in Olivgrün, doch wurde sie häufig gebleicht. Die Panzergranate 'AP40' wurde mit dem 50-mm-Geschütz L/42 eingesetzt. **H4** Die SS-Version der Panzeruniform—Winterausführung. Das Tragen der Mannschaften von Divisionsabzeichen auf beiden Kragenspiegeln gab es nur bei der 'Totenkopf'—Division. Der Mann hält ein Panzersprenggeschoß für das 50-mm-Geschütz L/60.